CONTENTS

WHAT IS A LIFE CYCLE?

All living things have a life cycle. They are all born, they all grow bigger, and their bodies change.

LIFE CYCLE OF A

KANGAROO

By Kirsty Holmes

KidHaven
PUBLISHING

LIFE CYCLES

Words that look like **this** can be found in the glossary on page 24.

Published in 2022 by
KidHaven Publishing, an Imprint of Greenhaven Publishing, LLC
353 3rd Avenue
Suite 255
New York, NY 10010

Edited by: Robin Twiddy
Designed by: Brandon Mattless

Cataloging-in-Publication Data

Names: Holmes, Kirsty.
Title: Life cycle of a kangaroo / Kirsty Holmes.
Description: New York : KidHaven Publishing, 2022. | Series: Life cycles | Includes glossary and index.
Identifiers: ISBN 9781534537903 (pbk.) | ISBN 9781534537927 (library bound) | ISBN 9781534537910 (6 pack) | ISBN 9781534537934 (ebook)
Subjects: LCSH: Kangaroos--Juvenile literature. | Kangaroos--Life cycles--Juvenile literature.
Classification: LCC QL737.M35 H68 2022 | DDC 599.2'22156--dc23

Printed in the United States of America

CPSIA compliance information: Batch #CSKH22: For further information contact Greenhaven Publishing LLC, New York, New York at 1-844-317-7404.

Please visit our website, www.greenhavenpublishing.com. For a free color catalog of all our high-quality books, call toll free 1-844-317-7404 or fax 1-844-317-7405.

PHOTO CREDITS

All images are courtesy of shutterstock.com, unless otherwise specified. With thanks to Getty Images, Thinkstock Photo and iStockphoto. Front cover & 1 – Edward Haylan, Bradley Blackburn 2- John Carnemolla 3 – Edward Haylan 4 – Paul Hakimata Photography, Oksana Kuzmina, S-F 5 – Monsterstock, Rido. Ljupco Smokovski 6 – Anan Kaewkhammul 7 – Luke Shelley 8 – Saran Jantraura 9 – Edwin Butters 10 – Katarina Christenson 11 – Belle Ciezak 12 – franco schettini 13 – Franzyy 14 – Andrey Bayda 15 – Anan Kaewkhammul, Bradley Blackburn, Edward Haylan 16 – Chris Watson 17 – Robert CHG 18 – Marina Kranina, Chris Watson, Bradley Blackburn 19 – Lucas T. Jahn, Gianna Stadelmyer, Johan Swanepoel 20 – Chris Watson, Edward Haylan, Picsfive 21 – Jason Cassidy, Chris Watson 22 – Edward Haylan, Susan Flashman, Saran Jantraura, MattLoves 23 – Edward Haylan, Kjuuurs, structuresxx, IntoTheWorld

When they are fully grown, they have **offspring** of their own. In the end, all living things die. This is the life cycle.

KICKING KANGAROOS

A kangaroo is a marsupial. Marsupials are mammals. Mammals give birth to live young and feed them milk. Marsupials have a special pouch for carrying their babies.

Kangaroos are mostly found in Australia and the islands around it.

Kangaroos have strong back legs and feet, and they get around by hopping and jumping. Large kangaroos can even use their long tails like a third leg to help them balance.

PERFECT PREGNANCY

Male kangaroos will fight over the females.

A female kangaroo **mates** with a male. The female is **pregnant** for about a month before she gives birth to a newborn baby, called a joey.

The newborn joey climbs toward the pouch and climbs inside. The joey **nurses** on the mother's milk and begins to grow.

The joey is pink, blind, and has no fur.

JOYFUL JOEYS

At first, the joey stays in the pouch as it grows its fur and opens its eyes. Its legs grow and get stronger, and its ears grow and start to stick up.

Can you see the baby joey in its mother's pouch?

Kangaroos look after their babies for a long time. The mother can get pregnant again while her first joey is still using the pouch. She makes different milk for each joey.

JUMPING JOEYS

The joey leaves the mother's pouch when it is a few months old. As it grows, it hops in and out of the pouch until it is big enough to leave forever.

Kangaroos live in groups called mobs. When a joey leaves the pouch for the last time, it becomes part of the mob. It still feeds on milk but also eats grass and leaves.

Kangaroos are herbivores. A herbivore is an animal that only eats plants.

KOOKY KANGAROOS!

Adult kangaroos are the only large animals that use hopping as their main way to move. Their big feet and strong legs help them jump a long way.

Some kangaroos can hop over 23 feet (7 m) in one jump!

Male kangaroos are called bucks. Female kangaroos are called does. There are lots of different **species** of kangaroos. Two of the best-known species are the gray kangaroo and the red kangaroo.

LIFE AS A KANGAROO

Lots of kangaroos are crepuscular. This means that they are most often seen just before the sun goes down or just after it comes up.

The largest male in a mob is known as the boomer.

Red kangaroos are the official **national animal** of Australia. Kangaroos are popular with tourists, who like to visit them and feed them.

FUN FACTS ABOUT KANGAROOS

- The red kangaroo is the largest living marsupial.

- The word "kangaroo" comes from an **Aboriginal** language. The word "gangurru" described the gray kangaroo.

• Kangaroos are good swimmers. On land they can only move their legs together, but in the water they can move them one at a time to swim.

Kangaroos are part of a group of animals called macropods. This means "long feet."

• Kangaroos cannot walk or hop backward.

THE END OF LIFE AS A KANGAROO

This older kangaroo has tattered ears.

Kangaroos can live for a long time. The giant red kangaroo can live for around 22 years. Gray kangaroos can live for around 12 years.

Kangaroos don't have many **predators**. They are good at fighting, and living in a mob helps keep them safe. Dingoes, which are a type of wild dog, will sometimes attack kangaroos.

Foxes and eagles will **prey on** joeys if they can.

THE LIFE CYCLE

The life cycle of a kangaroo has different stages. Each stage looks different from the last.

The newborn drinks its mother's milk and grows. Eventually, it will leave the pouch, become an adult, and start to have babies of its own.

GLOSSARY

Aboriginal	having to do with the native people of Australia – the first people to ever live in the country
mate	to make babies with another animal of the same type
national animal	an animal that has been chosen to represent a country
nurse	to drink milk
offspring	the young of an animal or plant
predator	an animal that hunts other animals for food
pregnant	describing a female animal has one or more young (babies) growing inside her
prey on	to hunt another animal for food
species	a group of very similar animals or plants that can create young together

INDEX